THE BOOK OF...

SPACE

KINGFISHER

KINGFISHER

First published 2013 by Kingfisher
an imprint of Macmillan Children's Books
a division of Macmillan Publishers Limited
20 New Wharf Road, London N1 9RR
Basingstoke and Oxford
Associated companies throughout the world
www.panmacmillan.com

Written and Illustrated by Dynamo Limited
Concept by Jo Connor

ISBN 978-0-7534-3644-8

Copyright © Macmillan Children's Books 2013

10 9 8 7 6 5 4 3 2 1
TTR/0413/LFG/UG/140MA

A CIP catalogue record for this book
is available from the British Library.

Printed in China

WHAT'S IN THIS BOOK?

SPACE...

HAVE YOU EVER WONDERED WHY... OR WHAT...OR WHEN?

It's only natural to wonder about the world around us. It's a very complicated and surprising place sometimes. And you'll never understand what is going on around you unless you ask yourself a question every now and again.

We have investigated the Universe to collect as many questions about space as we could find...

...and we also found the answers for you!

We now invite you to come with us on our journey around the Universe, so that we can show you all the answers we discovered.

While we were searching for all those answers, we found out some other pretty interesting things, too. We wrote them all down on these panels – so you can memorize these facts and impress your friends!

We also thought it might be fun to see how much of this shiny new knowledge you can remember – so at the back of the book, on pages 56 and 57, you'll find some Quick-Quiz questions to test you out. It's not as scary as it sounds – we promise it will be fun. (And besides, we've given you all the answers on pages 58 and 59.)

QUICK-QUIZ QUESTIONS

Are you ready for this big adventure?

Then let's go!

HOW FAR AWAY IS OUTER SPACE?

Outer space officially begins 100 kilometres above the ground at a spot called the Kármán line. Here the Earth's atmosphere, the blanket of air that surrounds the planet, thins out.

Did you know...

The Kármán line is the place where the air becomes too thin for ordinary aeroplanes to fly through it. Only super-fast rockets can travel this high.

WHAT IS SPACE MADE OF?

There are countless billions of stars, planets and moons in the Universe (the whole of space). There is also lots of mysterious stuff, known as dark matter, that we cannot see or touch. Scientists are only just beginning to learn about it and to find ways of measuring it.

Did you know...

We know there is invisible matter in space because we can measure its gravity (the force of it pulling on things), even though we can't see it.

Nobody is sure how old space is, but it could have begun between 10 and 20 billion years ago. It's possible that the Universe was born when a gigantic explosion called the Big Bang occurred, creating material and throwing it out in all directions.

Did you know...

After the Big Bang, the Universe probably cooled down, and material joined together to form the stars and planets.

HOW BIG IS SPACE?

End of space this way... maybe

Did you know...

Some scientists think that the Universe could be flat. Others think it could be round, like a ball, or curved, like a saddle.

Nobody knows how big the Universe is, because we cannot see to the edge. Using powerful telescopes, we can see as far as 14 billion light years from Earth (one light year measures 9,460,000,000,000 kilometres). We do not know how much further the Universe stretches.

DO STARS REALLY HAVE A SPIKY SHAPE?

Stars are not really pointy-shaped like star drawings are. They are giant balls of burning gas, and they only look spiky to us because of the way their light shimmers as it reaches us through the air in our atmosphere.

Did you know...

Stars are different sizes and colours. From Earth, an average-sized star looks yellow. A small star looks red and an extra-large star looks blue.

HOW COME THERE'S A BEAR IN SPACE?

Did you know...

People name constellations differently around the world. For instance, in the Marshall Islands in the North Pacific they don't see a Great Bear in the sky. They see a canoe instead.

The Great Bear and the Little Bear are star constellations. A constellation is a group of stars that people join together, like a join-the-dots puzzle, to make an imaginary picture in space.

IS THE MILKY WAY REALLY MILKY?

The Milky Way is a giant collection of stars and planets called a galaxy. It contains more than 200 billion stars and many planets, including Earth. In the night sky it looks like a thick, white band of stars, which is how it got its name.

Did you know...

The Milky Way's name comes from ancient times. The ancient Greeks called it 'the Milky Circle'. The Romans called it 'the Milky Road'.

IF STARS ARE SO BIG, WHY DO THEY LOOK SO SMALL?

Most stars are very far away from us, which is why they look so small. The nearest star to us is the Sun. It only looks larger and brighter than other stars because it is closer to us.

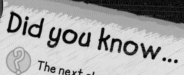

Did you know...

The next closest star to Earth is Proxima Centauri. It is about 4.3 light years (or 39,900,000,000,000 kilometres) away. A car travelling at an average speed would take more than 48 million years to reach it!

WHY DO STARS TWINKLE?

Stars don't really twinkle. They only appear to shimmer because the light they send out wobbles as it travels through the Earth's atmosphere to reach us.

HOW ARE STARS BORN?

Stars are born inside giant clouds of dust and gas called 'nebulas'. A star is formed when a particularly thick part of a nebula cloud collapses in on itself and heats up.

Did you know...

Newborn stars are called 'protostars'. It can take millions of years for a protostar to be born.

WHY DOES THE SUN DISAPPEAR AT NIGHT?

The Sun doesn't really disappear. Our planet spins as it travels around the Sun and, as the Earth turns, the part that faces away from the Sun has its night-time. Once it turns back towards the Sun, it has its daytime.

Did you know...

Because of the Earth's tilt, the areas around the North and South poles have six months of darkness in winter and six months of daylight in summer.

WILL THE SUN EVER STOP SHINING?

The Sun has been shining for about 4.6 billion years, and it will carry on shining for another 5 billion years. After that, it will run out of the fuel it uses to create heat and light.

Did you know...

The Sun itself is spinning. It takes roughly a month to turn around once, though the middle part of the Sun speeds around faster than the top and the bottom parts.

HOW FAST DOES THE EARTH SPIN?

Did you know...

The Milky Way is spinning through space, too. Scientists don't agree on the exact speed, but it could be around 530 kilometres a second.

The Earth spins around once in 24 hours, so the place where you are right now is moving at 1,675 kilometres per hour through space! That's 465 metres a second.

IF THE EARTH IS SPINNING, WHY DON'T WE FALL OFF?

We don't fall off because of gravity, which is the invisible force of attraction between objects. Earth has a very strong gravitational pull on us.

Did you know...

There is a gravitational pull between the Earth and the Sun, too, that keeps the Earth in orbit around the Sun.

WHY DO ASTRONAUTS SEEM TO FLOAT INSIDE SPACESHIPS?

Did you know...

Roughly half of all the astronauts who go into space suffer from space sickness – a bit like being car sick.

Astronauts are not really floating – they are falling. They hurtle at the same speed as their orbiting spacecraft, which is falling in a giant, curving path. Because the astronauts are falling at the same speed as their spacecraft, they seem to float.

WHY DO ASTRONAUTS NEED SPACE SUITS?

A space-walking astronaut would die quickly without a space suit. In space there is no air to breathe and no air pressure (on Earth, air pushes on your body and helps to keep it in shape). A suit provides air and air pressure, and also protects the body from freezing cold, boiling heat and dangerous radiation.

Did you know...

Without a space suit on, a space-walking astronaut would suffocate in about 15 seconds. His or her blood would boil and then freeze, and body parts such as the heart would explode.

WHAT CAN AN ASTRONAUT HEAR IN SPACE?

Sound is made by vibrations travelling through the air. Because there is no air in space, there is no sound. In space movies you might hear big explosions or crashes during noisy space battles, but these sounds are made up for effect. In reality, the sound would not travel.

Did you know...

Astronauts can hear each other talking inside their spacecraft, where there is plenty of air. Outside in space they can talk to each other through radios, but they cannot hear anything from outside their space suits.

WHAT WOULD HAPPEN IF AN ASTRONAUT BOILED WATER IN SPACE?

When air pressure is lower, water boils more quickly. Since there is no air pressure at all in space, the water would boil instantly, turn to steam and disappear.

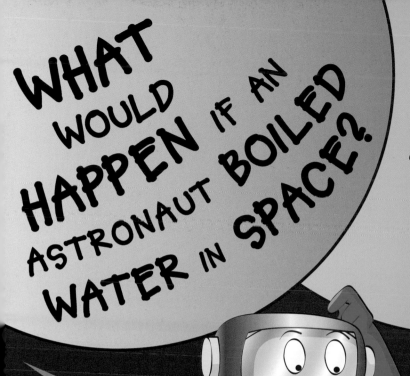

Did you know...

Water boils faster on top of a mountain than it does at sea level. Air is thinner high up on the mountain, so the air pressure is lower.

WHY ARE THERE VEHICLES PARKED ON THE MOON?

Space missions to the Moon left behind vehicles when the astronauts returned to Earth. American Apollo astronauts left behind three lunar rovers, which they drove around to pick up rock samples and explore the Moon's surface.

WHY DOES THE MOON LOOK SHINY?

The Moon does not make its own light. It looks shiny only because sunlight reflects off its surface.

Did you know...

The shadowy patches you can sometimes see on the Moon are its mountains and plains.

WHAT IS THE SOLAR SYSTEM?

The Solar System is the Sun and everything that orbits (travels around) it. There are eight planets in the Solar System, including Earth. There are also moons, asteroids and comets, all whizzing around the Sun.

Did you know...

In order, going away from the Sun, the planets in the Solar System are; Mercury, Venus, Earth, Mars, Jupiter, Saturn, Uranus and Neptune.

WHY ARE PLANETS DIFFERENT COLOURS?

A planet gets its colour from the way its surface and the atmosphere around it reflect sunlight. For instance, the Earth looks blue from space because it has so much water on its surface.

Did you know...

Venus is a yellowish colour and so is Saturn. Jupiter has white and orange bands around it and Mercury is grey. Mars is a rusty red, while Uranus and Neptune are shades of blue.

HAS MARS GONE RUSTY?

Mars is a red colour because its rocks are rusty. This is because they contain lots of rust particles, known scientifically as iron oxide.

Did you know...

Sometimes Mars has huge dust storms, when rusty particles of dust blow around and make the sky turn pink.

WHICH PLANET SPINS BACKWARDS?

Venus spins the opposite way to Earth. The Sun rises in the west and sinks in the east, the opposite of our planet. Venus spins very slowly – one full turn takes 243 Earth days.

Did you know...

The surface of Venus is covered in deadly, poisonous clouds and the temperature there is hot enough to melt lead.

WHY IS JUPITER SPOTTY AND STRIPY?

Through a telescope, Jupiter looks stripy, with a big red spot on its surface. The spot is a giant, whirling storm twice the size of Earth. The stripes are bands of different gases that surround the planet.

Did you know...

Jupiter is a huge ball of whirling gases and we do not know what is at the centre.

WHICH PLANET COULD FLOAT ON WATER?

If there was a body of water large enough, the planet Saturn would float in the water. This is because the gassy material it is made from is not as compacted as the material that makes water. So, even though the planet is massive, it is 'less dense' than water, which is why it would float.

Did you know...

Saturn's rings are made up of billions of pieces of ice, rock and dust whirling around the planet.

WHICH PLANET'S DAY LASTS FOR **58** EARTH DAYS?

A planet's day is the amount of time it takes to spin round once. Mercury spins slowly compared to Earth, and one day on Mercury lasts for 58.6 Earth days.

Did you know...

A year is the time it takes for a planet to orbit the Sun. A year on Mercury is very short – it lasts for just 88 Earth days.

WHICH PLANET IS TILTED ON ITS SIDE?

The planet Uranus is tilted on its side so that its poles (its top and bottom) face the Sun as it orbits. It is possible that it was once more upright like the Earth, but may have been knocked onto its side when it collided with something big in space.

Did you know...

Uranus takes 84 Earth years to go round the Sun. Because it is spinning while lying on its side, each of its poles is in daylight for 42 years, and in darkness for the next 42 years.

WHERE IS THE WINDIEST PLACE IN THE SOLAR SYSTEM?

Neptune has giant storms raging over its surface, with super-strong winds that have been measured at about 2,414 kilometres per hour – the fastest anywhere in the Solar System.

Did you know...

Neptune's storms were recorded and measured by a spacecraft called Voyager 2, which passed by the planet in 1989. It took 12 years to reach there from Earth.

IS PLUTO A PLANET?

Did you know...

Pluto is extremely cold because it is so far away from the Sun. It is probably made mostly of ice.

Pluto was once thought to be a full-sized planet, but now it is called a dwarf planet. This means it is too large to be an asteroid but too small to be a proper planet.

HOW DO PLANETS GET THEIR NAMES?

Did you know...

Uranus was once named 'Georgium', after the British king George the Third. It was renamed after the Greek god of the skies.

The planets in the Solar System are named after ancient Greek and Roman gods and goddesses. For instance, Venus was the Roman goddess of love, and Jupiter was the Roman king of the gods.

HOW DO PLANETS GET DISCOVERED?

Astronomers sometimes discover new planets by studying the data collected through powerful telescopes, which point at far-flung spots in the Universe. There are likely to be billions of planets so far undetected in space.

Did you know...

Planets look very dim and small compared to stars in the sky, so they are hard to find.

COULD WE GO ON HOLIDAY TO ANOTHER PLANET?

Most of the planets that we know of are surrounded by deadly, poisonous gases and are too hot or too cold. Mars could be visited by humans in the future, though, because there is water in the polar ice caps, and it is the most Earth-like planet in our Solar System.

Did you know...

It would probably take at least seven months for a crewed spaceship to reach Mars from Earth.

WHERE DO SPACE ALIENS LIVE?

We haven't found life in space yet, but with countless other planets and moons it seems likely that there will be some life somewhere. It might exist on another Earth-like planet orbiting its own star in a faraway galaxy.

Did you know...

Scientists constantly scan for signals that might have been sent from intelligent life somewhere else in the Universe.

WHERE IS THERE A BELT MADE OF ASTEROIDS?

Asteroids are lumps of rock ranging from the size of a pebble to 1,000 kilometres across. There are millions of asteroids in the Solar System, mostly orbiting the Sun in a doughnut-shaped ring called the Asteroid Belt, which lies between Mars and Jupiter.

Did you know...

In 2001, a spacecraft landed on an asteroid called Eros and took photos of its dry, rocky surface.

COULD HE RIDE ON A COMET'S TAIL?

Comets are made of ice, dust and fragments of rock. When a comet's orbit takes it near the Sun, some of the ice melts and dust and gas start to trail out behind in long, tail-shaped clouds. A comet can have two or three tails but they are not solid, so you couldn't sit on them.

Did you know...

Comet tails can stretch across space for millions of kilometres. Once a comet starts to head away from the Sun, the tails disappear.

WHY IS A SHOOTING STAR NOT REALLY A STAR?

Did you know...

At certain times of the year, the Earth passes through trails of debris left by orbiting comets. At these times you can see more meteors than usual in the night sky.

A shooting star is really a meteor – a small lump of space rock that burns as it falls through the Earth's atmosphere. As it glows, it looks like a streak of light in the night sky.

WHERE CAN WE FIND SPACE ROCKS ON EARTH?

Sometimes fragments of meteors, called meteorites, land on Earth. Most land in the sea, but the best place to find one is in a remote desert. Meteorites last longest here because they are untouched by rain, which tends to wear stones down after a while.

Did you know...

Between 30,000 and 80,000 meteorites fall to Earth every year.

WHY IS SPACE LIKE A JUNKYARD?

If you dropped something out in Earth's orbit, it would carry on whizzing around the planet as 'space junk'. Bits and pieces of old rockets and broken satellites are orbiting the Earth, as well as a wrench tool accidentally dropped by a US astronaut when he was out space-walking.

Did you know ...

There are roughly 13,000 fragments of space junk more than 10 centimetres wide orbiting the Earth.

DO COLLISIONS HAPPEN IN SPACE?

Chunks of space junk can collide and break up into smaller pieces. It's even possible that junk could hit a spacecraft. Scientists monitor the position of the junk, just in case of danger.

Did you know...

Most space junk eventually falls to Earth, burning up in the atmosphere.

IS A BLACK HOLE REALLY A HOLE?

A black hole is an area of space, usually in the middle of a galaxy, where gravity is so strong that it pulls everything in, even light. It is not really an empty hole. It is filled with material crammed into a very small space.

Did you know...

Material spirals towards a black hole like water going into a plughole.

WHERE CAN WE SEE A BLACK HOLE?

Did you know...

There is a black hole at the centre of our galaxy, but it is very far away from Earth and poses no danger.

We cannot see black holes because they don't give out any light. We know that they exist only because scientists can detect the heat and X-rays given out by the material spiralling into them.

IS SPACE FULL OF WORMHOLES?

There are lots of unproven theories about space, including the idea that there might be wormholes – tunnels in space that are shortcuts between two distant points in the Universe. Nobody knows if they really exist.

Did you know...

Wormholes could occur if space had curves and folds in it, but nobody knows if this is true.

COULD WE TRAVEL THROUGH WORMHOLES?

If wormholes existed it could be possible to travel through them to a part of the Universe that is in a different time. Science fiction (space story) writers have used this idea to put time travel in their stories.

Did you know...

Some astrophysicists (people who study space theories) have suggested that it might be possible to travel through a wormhole to different universes, next door to ours!

WHAT IS BIG, ROUND AND CAN SEE STARS?

Space telescopes can look deep into space to discover new objects such as stars and planets. Some telescopes are attached to spacecraft orbiting above the atmosphere, so they can get a clearer view of space than we do from Earth.

Did you know...

A space telescope has a giant, round mirror lens that gathers light from space. The biggest ones have lenses measuring more than six metres wide.

WHAT IS THE FURTHEST WE CAN SEE IN SPACE?

At the moment, space telescopes can see up to about 15 billion light years away, but bigger and more powerful ones are being designed all the time.

They transmit all the information they gather back to Earth for scientists to analyse.

Did you know...

The light that some telescopes pick up has taken billions of years to reach us.

WHAT DO WE THINK IS THE FASTEST THING IN SPACE?

Did you know...

Because the Sun is so far away from the Earth, its light takes about eight minutes to reach us.

As far as we know, light is the fastest thing in the Universe. One light year is the amount of distance light covers in one year. Light travels at 300,000 kilometres a second, the equivalent of several times around the Earth.

COULD ASTRONAUTS TRAVEL TO OTHER GALAXIES?

Most things in space are so far away from Earth that it would take an unimaginably long time to travel to them in a spaceship. It would not be practical for humans to go to other galaxies using the rockets we have today.

Did you know...

Robotic spaceships or 'space probes' can be sent over long distances, travelling for many years to reach faraway regions of space.

COULD WE LIVE IN SPACE ONE DAY?

Astronauts already live for long periods of time on board the International Space Station, orbiting the Earth. Their food and other supplies are brought up to them by rocket. In the future, it is possible that people could live in space permanently, perhaps inside a base on the Moon.

Did you know...

One day the Moon could be mined for its rocks, which could be shipped back to Earth in rockets launched from a Moon base.

WHAT IS IT LIKE TO LIVE IN SPACE?

Living in space causes problems for humans. The lack of gravity weakens the body's muscles, so astronauts have to exercise every day to stay strong. The fluids in the body tend to rise upwards, so astronauts get a stuffed-up feeling, as if they have a bad cold.

QUICK-QUIZ QUESTIONS

1. The Universe is three billion kilometres wide. True or false?

2. What is the name of our galaxy?

3. Which star is closest to Earth?

4. How long does it take the Earth to spin around once?

5. Is there sound out in space?

6. Is there wind on the Moon?

7. How many planets are there in the Solar System?

8. Which planet has red, rusty rocks?

9. Which planet spins the opposite way to Earth?

10. Is Jupiter a huge ball of gas or a huge ball of ice?

11. Which planet could float on water?

12. Mercury is the furthest Solar System planet from the Sun. True or false?

13. Which planet is tilted on its side?

14. Which is the stormiest planet in the Solar System?

15. Which dwarf planet used to be called a planet, but isn't any more?

16. Which planet is named after the Roman goddess of love?

17. Which planet is named after the Roman king of the gods?

18. Would you look out at faraway space using a microscope or a telescope?

19. How long would it take to travel to Mars in a spaceship?
a) 7 weeks; b) 7 months; c) 7 years.

20. What do we call the ring of asteroids orbiting the Sun?

21. What are comets made of?

22. What do we call a lump of space rock that has fallen to Earth?

23. Is it possible to see a black hole?

24. What is the fastest thing we know of in the Universe?

25. Humans could travel to other galaxies in spaceships. True or false?

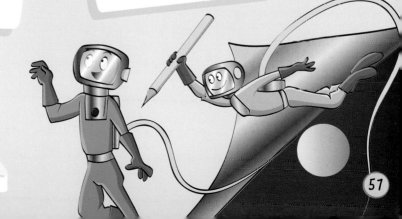

QUICK-QUIZ ANSWERS

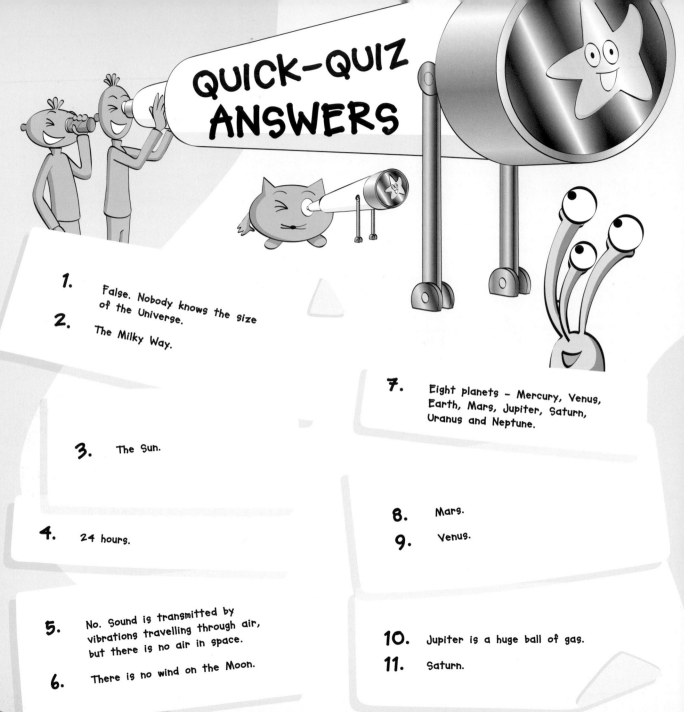

1. False. Nobody knows the size of the Universe.

2. The Milky Way.

3. The Sun.

4. 24 hours.

5. No. Sound is transmitted by vibrations travelling through air, but there is no air in space.

6. There is no wind on the Moon.

7. Eight planets – Mercury, Venus, Earth, Mars, Jupiter, Saturn, Uranus and Neptune.

8. Mars.

9. Venus.

10. Jupiter is a huge ball of gas.

11. Saturn.

12. False. It is the closest planet to the Sun.

13. Uranus.

14. Neptune.

15. Pluto.

16. Venus.

17. Jupiter.

18. A telescope.

19. b) at least 7 months.

20. The Asteroid Belt.

21. They are made of ice, dust and fragments of rock.

22. A meteorite.

23. No. Black holes do not give out any light, so they cannot be seen.

24. Light.

25. False. The galaxies are too far away.

TRICKY WORDS

AIR PRESSURE
The force of air pushing on something. On Earth we have air pressure pushing on us all the time. Out in space there is no air pressure.

ASTEROID
A large lump of rock orbiting a star.

ATMOSPHERE
The blanket of gases surrounding a planet. Earth's atmosphere contains the air that we breathe.

BIG BANG
A gigantic explosion of matter (stuff) that scientists think may have marked the beginning of space, time and everything.

BLACK HOLE
An area of space with a super-powerful gravitational pull.

COMET
A ball of ice, dust and rock fragments hurtling through space.

CONSTELLATION
A pattern in space, made by joining up a group of stars like a dot-to-dot picture.

DARK MATTER
Invisible material thought to make up most of the Universe.

DWARF PLANET
An object in space that is too small to be called a planet but too big to be called an asteroid.

GALAXY
A gigantic group of stars and planets, plus other dusty and gassy materials.

GAS PLANET
A planet that is made mostly of gases. Saturn, Jupiter, Uranus and Neptune are gas planets.

GRAVITY
A force of attraction between objects. This happens in space, for example, where a moon is held in orbit around a planet because the planet is more massive. This force is known as 'gravitational pull'. Big objects such as stars and planets have extra-strong pulling power.

LIGHT YEAR
The distance light travels in one year (about 10 trillion kilometres).

LUNAR
Anything to do with the Moon.

METEOR
A small lump of space rock falling downwards through the Earth's atmosphere (also known as a shooting star).

METEORITE
A fragment of space rock that has landed on Earth's surface.

MILKY WAY
The galaxy that contains the Sun, the Earth and the rest of the Solar System. It contains billions of other stars and planets, too.

NEBULA
A gigantic cloud of dust and gas in space. Stars are born in nebulas.

ORBIT
A journey around a star or a planet, for example. Earth is in orbit around the Sun.

PARTICLE
A very tiny piece of something.

PROTOSTAR
A baby star.

RADIATION
Energy that travels through space. Light and heat are both types of radiation.

REFLECTION
When light bounces off the surface of something.

SATELLITE
Something that orbits around something else. The Moon is Earth's natural satellite. Man-made satellites also orbit the Earth.

SCIENCE FICTION
Imaginary stories about space or the future.

SOLAR SYSTEM
The Sun and all the planets, moons and other objects that travel around it.

SPACE JUNK
Fragments of man-made space equipment, still orbiting the Earth long after they have become useless.

SPACE WALK
A period of activity outside a spacecraft, performed by an astronaut in space.

STAR
A giant ball of burning gas.

TELESCOPE
A piece of equipment used to see far into space.

VIBRATION
When something wobbles powerfully.

WORMHOLE
A shortcut in space between two places. Nobody knows if space wormholes really exist or not.

WHERE TO FIND STUFF

Wow! What an amazing journey! We hope you had as much fun as we did, and learnt many new things. Who knew there was so much to discover about Space! Here are some other exciting books where you'll find more to explore:

The Book Of... How?
The Book Of... What?
The Book Of... Where?
The Book Of... Which?
The Book Of... Who?
The Book Of... Why?
The Book Of... Animals
The Book Of... Dinosaurs
The Book Of... The Human Body

Look out for these great books! 'Who' knows 'what' we'll discover... See you soon!